TRAIN

BY ALEX SUMMERS

Rourke
Educational Media
rourkeeducationalmedia.com

Scan for Related Titles and Teacher Resources

Before & After Reading Activities

Teaching Focus:

Concepts of Print: Have students find capital letters and punctuation in a sentence. Ask students to explain the purpose for using them in a sentence.

Before Reading:

Building Academic Vocabulary and Background Knowledge

Before reading a book, it is important to set the stage for your child or student by using pre-reading strategies. This will help them develop their vocabulary, increase their reading comprehension, and make connections across the curriculum.

1. Read the title and look at the cover. *Let's make predictions about what this book will be about.*
2. Take a picture walk by talking about the pictures/photographs in the book. Implant the vocabulary as you take the picture walk. Be sure to talk about the text features such as headings, the Table of Contents, glossary, bolded words, captions, charts/diagrams, or Index.
3. Have students read the first page of text with you then have students read the remaining text.
4. Strategy Talk – use to assist students while reading.
   - Get your mouth ready
   - Look at the picture
   - Think…does it make sense
   - Think…does it look right
   - Think…does it sound right
   - Chunk it – by looking for a part you know
5. Read it again.

Content Area Vocabulary

Use glossary words in a sentence.

aboard
conductor
station
ticket

After Reading:

Comprehension and Extension Activity

After reading the book, work on the following questions with your child or students in order to check their level of reading comprehension and content mastery.

1. *Why do people ride trains? (Summarize)*
2. *Does a train have wheels? (Asking Questions)*
3. *If you could take a train somewhere, where would you go? (Text to self connection)*
4. *What does the conductor say when it is time to get on the train? (Asking Questions)*

Extension Activity

Different Kinds of Trains. There are trains that do other things besides carry people. With the help of an adult, see if you can find out what those trains do and what they carry. Make a list of the different types of trains and draw a picture of them. Do they look the same as a passenger train? How are they alike? How are they different?

Table of Contents

All Aboard!

Ready to go!

How will I get there?

SCHOOL BUS

I know! I will take a train. The train **station** is full of people.

ÜGOT
NOT IN SERVICE
First
185 129
2

Our train pulls into the station. I count the passenger cars. There are 30!

passenger cars
InterCity EXPRESS

The **conductor** says, "All **aboard!**" I give him my **ticket.**

ALL ABOARD!
conductor
welcome
Coachclass

Ready to Ride

I climb aboard.

I pick a seat by the window.

Some people are traveling to work. Not me! I am going shopping.

I look out the window.
Zoom! We are moving fast.

A train's wheels are called rail wheels.
They help the train stay on the track.

track

The train stops.
The doors open.

doors

I'm here!

Picture Glossary

aboard (uh-BORD): To get on or onto a train, ship, or aircraft.

conductor (kuhn-DUHK-tur): A person who collects tickets on a train.

station (STAY-shuhn): A place where tickets for trains and buses are sold.

ticket (TIK-it): A ticket is a printed piece of paper that lets you go into a place, such as inside a train.

Index

Websites to Visit

http://easyscienceforkids.com
http://play.thomasandfriends.com/en-us/games
http://play-trains.com

About the Author

Alex Summers enjoys all forms of transportation. Especially if they are taking her to places she has never been or seen before. She loves to travel, read, write, and dream about all the places she will visit someday!

Meet The Author!
www.meetREMauthors.com

Library of Congress PCN Data

Train / Alex Summers
(Transportation and Me!)
ISBN 978-1-68342-163-4 (hard cover)
ISBN 978-1-68342-205-1 (soft cover)
ISBN 978-1-68342-232-7 (e-Book)
Library of Congress Control Number: 2016956592

Rourke Educational Media
Printed in the United States of America,
North Mankato, Minnesota

Also Available as:
ROURKE'S e-Books

www.rourkeeducationalmedia.com

Edited by: Keli Sipperley
Cover design by: Tara Raymo
Interior design by: Rhea Magaro-Wallace
Photo Credits: Cover © IKlein; page 5 © Andresimaging, scanrail, eyeware, Gugurat; page 6 © David Graham86; page 9 © scanrail; page 11 © AmericanSpirit; page 12, 20 © DenBoma; page 15 © Monkey Business Images; page 16 © Maria Pavola; page 18 © Karinclaus; page 22 © Andresimaging